I KNOW IN AND OUT

By Rosie Banks

Gareth Stevens
PUBLISHING

first concepts

Directions tell us
the way to go.

In and out are directions.

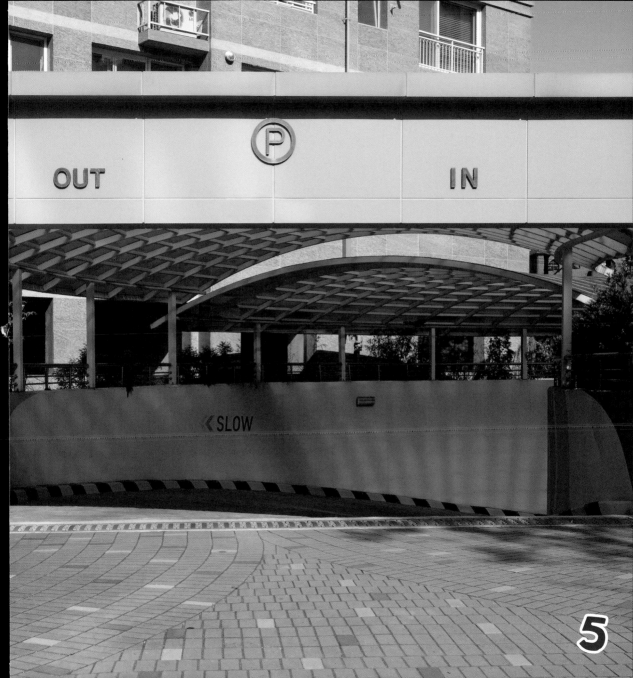

The cars drive in.

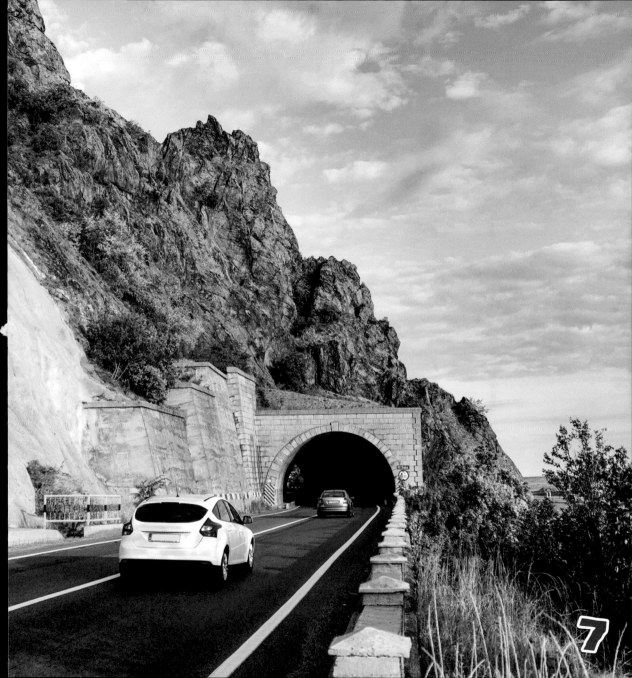

The cars drive out.

The penguin jumps in.

The penguin jumps out.

13

The kids walk in.

The kids walk out.

The kitten is
in the basket.

19

The kitten is
out of the basket.

I can go
in and out too!

Please visit our website, www.garethstevens.com. For a free color catalog of all our high-quality books, call toll free 1-800-542-2595 or fax 1-877-542-2596.

Cataloging-in-Publication Data
Names: Banks, Rosie, 1978- author.
Title: I know in and out / Rosie Banks.
Description: New York : Gareth Stevens Publishing, [2023] | Series: I know directions | Includes index.
Identifiers: LCCN 2022021750 (print) | LCCN 2022021751 (ebook) | ISBN 9781538282816 (library binding) | ISBN 9781538282793 (paperback) | ISBN 9781538282823 (ebook)
Subjects: LCSH: Orientation–Juvenile literature.
Classification: LCC BF299.O7 B35 2023 (print) | LCC BF299.O7 (ebook) | DDC 152.1/882–dc23/eng/20220614
LC record available at https://lccn.loc.gov/2022021750
LC ebook record available at https://lccn.loc.gov/2022021751
First Edition

Published in 2023 by
Gareth Stevens Publishing
2544 Clinton Street
Buffalo, NY 14224

Copyright © 2023 Gareth Stevens Publishing

Designer: Leslie Taylor
Editor: Therese Shea

Photo credits: Cover, p. 1 (stripes) Eky Studio/Shutterstock.com; cover (prairie dog in) AlessandroZocc/Shutterstock.com; cover (prairie dog out) erce Almoguera Haro/Shutterstock.com; p. 3 Kanchana P/Shutterstock.com; p. 5 Johnathan21/Shutterstock.com; p. 7 Bogdan Vacarciuc/Shutterstock.com; p. 9 Bogdan Vacarciuc/Shutterstock.com; p. 11 robert mcgillivray/Shutterstock.com; p. 13 rooh183/Shutterstock.com; p. 15 LStockStudio/Shutterstock.com; p. 17 Inside Creative House/Shutterstock.com; p. 19 Ivonne Wierink/Shutterstock.com; p. 21 Ivonne Wierink/Shutterstock.com; p. 23 New Africa/Shutterstock.com.

Printed in the United States of America

CPSIA compliance information: Batch #CWGS23: For further information contact Gareth Stevens, New York, New York at 1-800-542-2595.